THE SPIRIT OF
GARDENING

Nancy Mair

THE SPIRIT OF
GARDENING

Nancy Mair

Crystal Clarity Publishers
Nevada City, California

ISBN 1-56589-204-6

1 3 5 7 9 10 8 6 4 2

Design by Stephanie Steyer
Cover design by Lisa Lenthall and Stephanie Steyer
Photography by Barbara Bingham, Jyotish Novak, Jeffrey Philpott,
Kathleen Rainbow and Stephanie Steyer
Illustrations by Karen White
Special thanks to Weiss Brothers Nursery in Nevada City, CA

Crystal Clarity Publishers
14618 Tyler Foote Road
Nevada City, CA 95959
Phone: 800.424.1055 or 530.478.7600
E-mail: clarity@crystalclarity.com
Website: www.crystalclarity.com

Printed in China

Library of Congress Cataloging-in-Publication Data
Mair, Nancy.
The spirit of gardening / Nancy Mair.
p. cm.
ISBN-13: 978-1-56589-204-0
1. Gardening. 2. Gardens. 3. Gardening—Pictorial works.
4. Gardens—Pictorial works. I. Title.
SB455.M3663 2005
635.9'022'2—dc22
2005004616

Dedicated to J. Donald Walters,
with my deepest gratitude.

CONTENTS

The Essence of a Garden

The essence of gardening is creating and caring for a garden that is personally fulfilling—a garden that reflects what you wish to feel inside, uplifts your spirit, and becomes a haven offering you sanctuary and happiness.

The size of your garden doesn't matter—whether it's grand in scale or a tiny plot of land. Maybe all you have is a balcony to make into your garden. The spirit you instill in your garden is what counts, and will then be reflected back to you and others.

When in touch with this spirit of gardening, you gain a greater awareness of life through flowers, trees, and shrubs, and through shaping the earth and caring for the soil. You create more balance and harmony in your life through your surroundings, so *you* can grow and flourish. This spirit of gardening bestows an expansive, inspiring approach to all of life.

In the long-cherished story, *The Secret Garden*, a walled garden has been locked away. The buried key is found by a little girl named Mary. In time, Mary brings two new-found friends into the secret garden (along with the gruff, old gardener). Through loving care, toil, and the spirit of discovery within the garden and themselves, the garden is restored to a state of beauty and inspiration.

This enlightening story beautifully illustrates the principles of the spirit of gardening. Each child has a unique approach to the garden and way of uncovering its beauty. They each learn, grow, and thrive physically and emotionally in the process, and are rejuvenated deep in the heart of their beings. Who they become, and how they relate to other people and all of life, is heightened by their experiences. And finally, as the story ends, the children's life-changing perceptions in the garden help them bring greater happiness and transformation to others.

So, how does one create a garden, and experience this ideal spirit in real life?

TWO

Where to Begin?

There is no set formula as to where you *must* begin in your yard or garden. Simply start with **what is most important to you.** That way your heart will be in what you do.

Make a list that includes all that you want in your garden. Is it a play area for children; a nice entryway to your home; a vegetable garden, herb bed, a few fruit trees or an orchard; a nice garden to sit in, or view from a window; or privacy from neighbors or a road? Do you want to be surrounded by greenery, or greeted by colorful flowers; wish for a garden spot for birds or butterflies; a pond for frogs, fish, or waterlilies; trees for children or cats to climb, or to provide shade on hot summer days; a nice and secure place for dogs to

run and play, or a treehouse where children can gather? Are you needing a place to entertain friends or have family gatherings? Or are you longing for a personal refuge, a quiet place for contemplation or meditation?

Now prioritize your list, so the most meaningful items can become your initial focus. In gardens, you usually can't do just one aspect without including some others, but at least this will give you a place to start and bring clarity to the process.

THREE

The Four Elements

Physical, Mental, Emotional, and Spiritual

There are four aspects to our being: physical, mental, emotional, and spiritual. These can also be represented in the garden: The physical features; the mental elements of design, function, and interest; the emotional feeling of the garden;

and the spiritual place for inspiration. Look at what aspects are strongest in *you*, for that is what you will relate to most easily. I'll give a few examples:

A person who is very physical—does a lot of sports, loves exercise, always wants to be on the move—may want the garden or yard to have features that allow for physical activities or sports. Is there room to play volleyball, croquet, basketball, or to swim? What would you like to *do* at home? How about a workshop? The physical act of working in the garden—pruning, planting, weeding, raking, and composting—may also be very fulfilling.

A mental, logical, or intellectual person may enjoy the visual lines of a garden more than flowers, or like a feature that sparks curiosity or observation. The garden will need to appeal to the mind—with an orderly or methodical layout, practical things, or elements that make sense. Look at the elements of your lifestyle and what garden features fit in with that, as well as what interests you, like a vegetable or herb garden, statuary or art, stonework, or organic gardening and composting. If your real thrill is in propagating plants, a greenhouse may be the perfect "garden" for you, where you can spend time in a controlled environment with your projects. Also, practical items, like an automatic watering system, may be greatly appreciated.

A feeling, emotional, or intuitive person will want the garden to *feel* good to them: peaceful, happy, abundant, exotic, relaxing, playful, and so on—or express numerous feelings. If this is your nature, what flowers, shrubs, or trees do you like, make you feel good, or evoke fond memories? Did your mother, father, sibling, grandparent, or friend have a favorite flower or garden feature that you would like to include around your own home? And, also important, are there plants or elements with *un*pleasant memories that you want to avoid?

The spiritually-oriented person will value a garden with qualities that uplift the spirit, expand awareness, and are reminders of a higher consciousness or the Divine. This garden may express higher aspirations such as inner peace, expansiveness, light, joy, harmony, or divine love. The design may be filled with light, beauty, and a sense of grace; flow towards a soaring, expansive

view; reflect simplicity, or a tranquil beauty; incorporate statues as reminders of the divine reality; or include an area for meditation or contemplation. Fluid lines, sweeps of color, harmony through varying shapes and hues, and graceful trees or arches are uplifting to behold and enhance the spiritual vision.

Of course, a person is more than just physical, or mental, or emotional, or spiritual. The combi-

nation and strength of each quality is what makes each person, and each garden, unique.

Also, if two people are creating a garden together, you can see that what is very important to one person may have little significance to another. Select features that will make the garden fulfilling for both of you.

There are four
aspects to
our being:
physical, mental,
emotional, and
spiritual.

FOUR

Physical Needs and Emotional Comforts

Now that you have your list of items, and understand a little of why some things will be more important to one person than to another, it's time to narrow down what will come first.

There are two aspects I take into account when helping someone improve or create their garden. The physical aspects or needs are one part. The emotional part, or what will feel good to the person or people living there, is the other. The emotional aspect includes what is *important* and *fulfilling* for the physical, mental, emotional, or spiritually-inclined person.

The physical aspect includes the structures and non-plant elements, or "hardscape," as it is called. These are the parts of the garden that are not living, breathing, and requiring nourishment. This includes paths and walkways; patios, decks, and arbors; fences or walls; terraces or raised beds of wood, stone, concrete, or stucco; water features such as a pond, waterfall, fountain, hot tub, or swimming pool; and a greenhouse, gazebo, or any structure attached to or separate from the house. I think of the hardscape as anything I can't dig up with a trowel or shovel.

Are there physical elements that can be added or changed to make your garden a better extension of your lifestyle at home? Maybe an arbor will give you the shade you need in order to sit outside and enjoy the summer's days and evenings, or provide a nicer place for grilling your meals? Or do you really want a hot tub to soak in and unwind at the end of a long day?

The other necessary aspect is how you want your garden to FEEL. When you first enter your yard or garden, or step onto the pathway to your door, is your first response, "Ah... it feels good to be home again!"

A garden should support your feelings or emotional life at home. The way your garden feels may be vastly more important to you than the physical elements. Create a place in the garden where you will *feel* good, and will like to spend time enjoying your home life.

Is having privacy and time alone a main concern—creating a place where you feel protected or sheltered from the demands of the outside world and the eyes of neighbors? If so, then start with how to create privacy: where to plant a tree, shrubs, or vines, or build some form of screen, fence, wall, or building that will provide what is important to you.

Your sense of well-being is the most vital of all. You may have a clear idea of the physical features you'd like, or you may know more clearly the mood or feeling you want your garden to have. Begin with what is most natural to you. The rest can unfold from those beginnings.

If you always remember to regard your garden according to your own nature, and combine that with the direction you want your garden to take, you will experience the spirit of gardening come to life.

Create a place in
the garden where
you will feel good,
and will like to
spend time enjoying
your home life.

The Landscape Design

The Outlines of a Garden

There are basic elements of design that create the shapes, flow, and specific areas in a garden. These physical elements are areas such as walkways, steps, decks, patios, trellises, terraced and raised beds, and ponds or pools. The

term "hardscape" is favored by many professionals, and includes all the areas requiring construction work, or the non-plant parts of a garden. However, using the word "landscape" seems much nicer to me, and includes all the construction features, along with the soil and plants, encompassing the whole experience of a garden.

Designing Your Garden

Creating a design flow that works for you and your lifestyle, as well as with the house or building, is where the art of garden design begins. The basic shapes usually start with the physical elements that allow people to go from one place to another, rather than the plantings. I normally

start a garden design by establishing where people want to walk, then create the rest of the landscape from there.

Walkways and Paths

Walkways are one of the most-used features in a garden. You may already have walkways that you don't want to change, but if you are creating a new garden or developing an area, then start with pathways for accessibility.

Walkways are your guides. They are meant to provide safe and easy passage to and from your home. Walkways guide people to the front door of the house, and possibly to a kitchen or back entrance, around the sides of the house, and out to a garage or parking area. Ideally, they are comfortable to walk along both day and night, and direct people clearly to their destination.

I learned a simple technique that exemplifies the inspired garden design. This will give you walkways and paths that you'll love to use, just where you want them.

George Washington Carver, the famous botanist and agriculturist who is perhaps best known for having discovered hundreds of uses for the peanut (including peanut butter!), also discovered the secret to creating the perfect pathway. He was designing the campus landscape at Tuskegee Institute in Alabama, where he was Director of Agriculture. He carefully laid out the grounds for a park-like setting, with paths leading to the various buildings. The students and faculty, however, ignored the walkways and his signs, and trod across the fragile young grass when heading to their classes and dormitories. Professor Carver puzzled over this problem for a while, then suddenly understood. For a few days he watched where the students and faculty walked, and then changed the location of the paths accordingly, placing the new walkways

"under their feet," right where they had been walking. From then on, everyone stayed on the pathways and the grass flourished.

And that, really, is *the key* to walkways and paths. Put them where people want to walk—not just where you think they should be. We have probably all been in a park or parking lot where people have worn a path between the shrubbery by taking a more direct route to their destination. I've taken those shortcuts myself! People cut through the bushes because that is the natural walking flow. The bushes are simply in the wrong place—they are where the walkway should have gone. And the same principle is true in your garden.

Allow yourself to go where you want to go. If you already have your walkways, there may be a spot where people tend to cut a corner, or take a shortcut. Rather than try to force people to stay on the walk with plantings, make room for them to follow the natural route. Provide stepping stones or a nice, firm surface for them to use so their shoes stay clean and dry where they take their alternate course.

As to where walkways should be, at the very least, I think it essential to have a main walkway

Creating a design
flow that works for
you and your
lifestyle... is where
the art of garden
design begins.

between the street and the front door of the house, and to where cars are parked. But there is no reason for this to look boring, with the same design from house to house. Each walkway has a distinctive width, length, shape, and surface material. In your setting, and with the design of your house, you might prefer an alternative to the traditional shape of walkway. At entryways where it is obvious how to reach the front door, a large patio, deck, or area of crushed hard-packed stones or gravel, will allow people to take whatever route they like, and works as a great alternative to the more defined walk.

Other than the main entries, you don't *need* to have a formal path under your feet. It's up to you —how much you walk around your garden, the style of garden you like (formal or informal), and if your climate requires secure, firm surfaces for safety and to keep feet dry.

In areas other than the main thoroughfares you can be more casual in your approach. Some open garden areas are nice to walk across without having a defined course. Lawn makes a pleasurable surface for walking and can be used as an informal avenue through the garden. The shredded or "mini" size landscape bark also makes a cushiony walking surface, with a natural woodland appearance around trees and shrubs. Both lawn and bark can be used to cover broad areas, as well as garden paths.

Destinations You Enjoy

George Washington Carver's discovery leads to more than pathways—it extends to the *entire layout* of a landscape. We know to put paths where people want to walk, but his same concept applies to every destination in the garden. Put your areas of activity where you like spending time. Decks and patios should be placed where people naturally gravitate, and any destination in the garden—a dining area, gazebo, green-house, shed, play area, swimming pool—in areas where people *like* to be. Then fill in the areas where people are *not* inclined to walk or linger with your plantings, or anything pleasing to look at. The idea is to work with the energy or magnetism of a space, and not expect it to be other than it is.

The concept of selecting a magnetic place is very familiar to the business world. A good location for a business is vital, and one of the first consid-erations when establishing a place of business.

Some locations, people seem to love going to. Whereas others—well, every business fails that moves in there. If a location has had several failed businesses, then no wise business person will risk that spot. It takes more than good parking, and a lot of traffic going by, to draw people into a place of business. It comes down to the energy of a place or location, which is easier to tell in a garden than out on the city streets.

In a garden, you can walk around to see and feel for yourself the places you like to walk, and the places you like to linger. You can also observe the areas where others seem to be drawn. Feeling the energy of a space may sound esoteric, and is easier for some people to do than it is for others —but the more you try, the more you can develop this talent of feeling and noticing the energy of your garden spaces.

Start by asking yourself, where do you like to go when you step outside the house and go into the garden? Look around. Is there already a place you like to sit or relax? Are there places where you and others never seem to go? If you have children, watch to see where they go to play—close to the house, over in a corner, in the middle of the yard? Their favorite places will probably be good play areas for them, or places for your activities, too.

Walk around your garden to see and feel all the spaces. Take your time, allowing yourself to slow down and notice. Feel which areas you want to keep walking through, and which seem to be nice places to pause in for a while.

Also consider how you plan to use the areas. Are you thinking of creating a vegetable garden? Which part of your garden is nice to walk to from the house (for harvesting vegetables, and tending the plants)? You need to like going there, as well as enjoy the feeling of the space itself. Are you wanting an outdoor space for cooking or dining?

Add your personal
touch to create a
garden that is
uplifting to you.

Walk from the house to the spot you are considering. Think about how it will work to get food and table-settings out there from the kitchen. Does the physical flow work? Would another spot have a smoother flow?

The distance you walk doesn't matter as much as the walking flow to the space. If there are a lot of corners, or other types of obstructions, then the location will feel more awkward. The physical flow from the house to the outside area is *very* important. This is the main pattern for going somewhere: from house to garden. Walk to and from the area to see if you are happy with your choice. The flow between the house and the area in the garden has to feel good, and the area where you plan to spend time needs to feel like a nice place to be. Otherwise, the place may look inviting—but people won't go there.

If you have more than one area to develop (like a vegetable garden *and* a dining area), then also see that there is a pleasing flow between those two spaces and the house. A good garden design is like a good house design. In a well-designed house, the rooms have a good flow from one to the other, and all of the rooms are nice to spend time in. Make the same true in your garden.

Once you establish the areas that will have a purpose, all the remaining spaces can then be designed to enhance those basic forms. Fill in the garden with beauty and interest. Use plantlife in its various forms of trees, shrubs, flowers, vines, groundcovers, and lawn. Add a fountain, stream, pond, or waterfall. Include artworks or statuary if that is your fancy, or create an area for wild birds. Make the remaining spaces into *visual* assets, rather than practical places to be. You need these areas of beauty, as well as the places with a purpose. Add your personal touch to create a garden that is uplifting to you.

SIX

A Garden With Style

Just as each person is a unique individual, each garden is unique. For a garden to enhance your life, it needs to reflect who you are, who you want to become, and include aspects of other people who live in your home. Of course, the garden area will also have its own energy, and by being sensitive to the site, the land will "tell" you what is wanting to happen, and what feels or looks right.

Gardens have style and personalities. Some are formal and structured, others cozy and flowery. Some are playful while others may be quite serious. A garden may be glorious with color; quiet and contemplative; simple and elegant; and reflect virtually any personality and style traits that a person may have.

How do gardens get these personalities? What makes some gardens seem exactly right—a pleasure to see and experience? And how do you create one?

An inspiring garden with style and personality has four main qualities: it complements the design of your home or building; is harmonious with your environment; reflects your own nature and lifestyle; and is uplifting to you, reflecting your highest aspirations.

Harmony from House to Garden

The design of a garden depends in large part on the architectural features of the home.

Houses made of concrete, steel, and glass, with square or odd-shaped windows, sharp edges and abrupt corners, sleek modern lines, and hard, shiny surfaces, have more of an intellectual presence. This type of dwelling is often surrounded by

A great garden
will integrate and
connect with the
shapes, colors,
materials used, and
architectural style
of the house.

landscaping aimed at captivating the mind with contours, shapes, and lines, rather than featuring the soft beauty of flowers. In fact, it would look quite ridiculous to have a house composed of lines and angles surrounded by a

house, a grand Italian villa, or a suburban neighborhood house waiting for its individuality to come forth?

landscape designed after a cozy English cottage garden, with flowerboxes trailing colorful tendrils and flowerbeds filled with a mingling array of soft pink roses, scented violets, and variously hued perennials. The bold, crisp lines of the house wouldn't relate to the quaintness of the garden.

A dwelling with arched windows and doorways, domed ceilings, plaster walls, and corners that are slightly rounded offers a more feminine design. The garden will do well to elaborate on that style or feeling in some way.

Really look at the style and architecture of your house. What style of garden will work with its architectural details? Does your home have the look or feeling of a cottage in the woods, a Mission- or ranch-style house, a French country

If the architecture has distinctive characteristics, then your design will probably be best if it acknowledges that heritage to some extent. However, if the house has a more conventional shape and features, then you will have a wider variety of garden styles that will blend with the home. Whichever situation you have, as you work with your garden, continue to view the plantings and layout with how they connect to the home.

If you love the lively interplay and mix of blooms of an English cottage garden, but that theme doesn't go well with the architecture of your home, pick out certain elements that *will* work. Will the dignified spires of delphinium go with your home? Can you incorporate a climbing rose or scented vine near an entryway? Will a carefree mix of lupines and violets fit into a cozy nook? Or is there some place a mass of forget-me-nots will flourish? Think about what says "English cottage garden" to you, and use what will harmonize with the architecture of your home.

A great garden will integrate and connect with the shapes, colors, materials used, and architectural style of the house. What texture and materials make up the sides of your house? Is it stucco, wood, brick, stone, concrete, steel, glass, or adobe? Look around for other houses with a similar siding and architecture that have a garden design with characteristics that you would like. What features are most attractive in those gardens—the curving or straight paths, the abundance or minimal amount of flowers, the materials used in walkways or patios, the style of plantings or shapes of flowerbeds? Integrate the elements you admire into your own garden.

Select landscape materials for your pathways, fence, gate, deck, and patio that flatter or blend with the home, and give the effect you wish to create. For instance, if the house is very formal in appearance, you will probably want the surface of your walkways to give a formal impression. If your home looks quite modest, a grand or elaborate walkway will be overpowering. Allow the personality of the house to blend with, or be

enhanced by, the garden. One or the other can be predominant, either the house or the garden, but they still need to live in harmony together. The relationship between the two should always be supportive.

Think about what resonates with your home, not just what's in fashion. When the whole garden-and-home environment is in harmony, and also reflects who you are, it will have the appearance of being a natural extension of yourself. People who visit will think, "This feels just like my friend!"

Be in Harmony with the Environment

The natural terrain and type of environment is another fundamental guide to the style of your garden. You have to work with what you have.

A hillside landscape will most likely need to be retained or terraced to create flat areas for plantings and usable outdoor areas. On steeper slopes, you may want to form tiers down the hill by building formal terraces, or create a flowing series of smaller beds in various sizes—what I call pocket beds. Also, groundcover or shrubs may be planted to soften the look of the terrain, and to secure the topsoil.

A moderate slope offers a visual flow that adds interest and variety. This can be shaped into different usable levels or integrated "as is" into the garden design.

A gentle grade gives you the freedom to easily plant the entire landscape, and contour the ground as you wish. A change in elevations gives you exciting ways to create visual depth with your plantings, and a sense of curiosity about what lies ahead.

A flat piece of land often benefits from some contouring. Shapes and forms can be added by mounding soil, or building raised beds of whatever height goes with your style of house and garden. Along with sculpting the land, add features that will give the eye something to focus upon. A fountain, a decorative wall, an archway or arbor, trees, hedges, and other features with vertical shapes, will give the garden depth and increase the allure. Areas such as a gazebo, trellis-covered deck, and other outdoor destinations are additional ways to bring in visual details, as well as bring you places to enjoy the outdoors.

The Borrowed Landscape

What lies beyond the boundaries of your garden? What do you see above fencelines, in neighboring yards, or off in the distance? Can you incorporate this "borrowed landscape" into your garden design? Neighboring trees often lend their height, color, and structure to portions of one's garden. Vines and flowering shrubs can be other welcome sights. It is very convenient when the neighbor's trees, foliage, and structures are beautiful or intriguing to behold, and add their attractiveness to your field of vision. Then you can incorporate the structure, colors, and shapes of the nearby landscape into the design of your own garden. Treat them as though *you* planted or placed them there.

When the nearby landscape is *not* so nice to see, then try to create a visual screen if you can, or draw attention away from that spot with something more magnetic in your own space. If you can't divert attention away from the unattractive flora or structure, then you may want to mirror its shape, color, or the materials it's made from, somewhere in your personal design. That way the nearby offense is not emphasized even more by its total exclusion. If you can't move it, or change it, then you have to work with what's there.

Property with a view brings a feeling of expansiveness to your setting. A vista of hills or mountains, a verdant valley, open fields, forest, or expanse of open water adds greatly to the magnetism of the landscape.

There are two main ways to treat a view. One, is to treat the garden like a separate, defined space, with the view a distant landscape. This style gives you the feeling of a garden oasis, amidst the surrounding scenery. With this style, you can use the colors, flowers, trees, and design shapes you like. Then the eye will go from your garden oasis to the expansiveness of the view beyond. In this type of design, it is nice to have some kind of definition at the point where the eye leaves your garden and shifts to the view. A border or horizontal feature will visually contain your garden, and give a last focal point before the vista beyond. Use a low-growing hedge, border of flowers, a deck railing, a low wall or fence, or whatever can easily be incorporated into your landscape design.

The other method of working with a view is to have your garden be an extension of, or mirror,

the surroundings. If you have green rolling hills or parkland that you see from your place, then you can plant your garden with a similar greenery and contouring to make it look as though your garden is a part of the surrounding scenery. If water is in the distance, you can create a pool at the edge of your garden that visually connects with the distant water, as though one leads to the other. If rocky hills are in the distance, then rocks with a similar texture and color in your garden will seem to connect the two areas. Essentially, whatever makes up your view, include in your garden—especially in your line of sight before you look out to the expanse beyond.

Whichever method you choose, it is always pleasing to pick up some of the colors that are in the distance, and include them in your garden. This is especially enchanting if your view includes the first rays of sunrise or the glowing colors at sunset. Flowers or foliage that mirror the colors in the sky and on the horizon will bring a magical feeling to your garden during those special times of day. Yellows will emphasize sunlight and dawn's early rays. For evening views, have flowers in rosy hues, lavender shades, peaches, soft oranges, pinks, and shades of blue to cover the spectrum of colors as the day slowly fades into night.

Let Your Spirit Reflect in the Garden

What kind of style can a backyard, driveway, vegetable patch, or front entry have? First, take time to consider YOU. Just as each person has distinctive qualities, each garden has a distinctive personality or energy. The aspects of ourselves that people see at work or in social situations can't reveal all our qualities. At home, we can express other interests and sides to ourselves. What direction do you want your garden to take? What do you want the garden to do for you, and for others?

Do you want to feel comforted and nurtured at home in your garden, or be surrounded by color and life? Are you seeking a serene refuge, a tranquil place where you can feel restored within? Create that environment around your home.

You can enhance a quality you already have, or balance it with another. If you have a lively personality, do you want to emphasize your lively nature by creating a vibrant garden filled with energy? Or do you feel a need to bring balance to your lively on-the-go disposition, and surround yourself in a calming environment? Choose what works for you.

Would you like the garden to represent a quality you wish to be surrounded by, or develop and encourage in yourself? Peace, light, calmness, an attitude of expansiveness towards all of life, a nurturing and giving nature—think about how you can bring that into your garden.

Peace can be inspired by peaceful colors, and a garden that embraces you with its beauty or simplicity. Include graceful lines in the plantings. Create pathways with fluid, gentle curves for a sense of movement, and soften hard edges with color or the texture of foliage.

Light can be allowed to fill your garden, and come streaming into your home to add lightness to your heart and spirit. Use colors in flowers, foliage, and structures that give you the sense of light that you seek.

Calmness can be conveyed in a garden where you can quietly work the soil, sit without interruption, and take the time to breathe deeply in the fresh air. Simply feeling the earth with your hands, planting, pruning, weeding, fertilizing, or composting, can be very grounding and calming to the body's energy. Green is a very soothing color. Incorporate layers of green foliage if you wish to feel more embraced and comforted by your surroundings. A little time in the garden can help dissolve away many of the tensions of the day. And the inner qualities of love and tenderness, a caring and giving attitude, and an attunement to Nature can unfold in the careful tending of plants and caring for a garden.

A playful spirit is nice to let show in some way, if that is your nature, for it brings smiles and laughter. Maybe the playfulness is expressed with a treehouse, a rope swing, a delightful garden sculpture or piece of art, amusing wind chimes or mobiles, or fun things to do in the garden.

Consider what qualities you want your garden to have, and include that feeling, or some visual reminder, in every part of your garden. The spirit of the garden is an expression of your life.

A Time of Day

If you are a morning person, look at the light in your garden in the early hours, and place flowers, shrubs, or trees that pick up the beautiful golden light of sunrise in the fall, the pearly light of winter mornings, or summer's clear yellow glow. Select leaf colors that you especially enjoy, place favorite flowers or a tree where the first light will make it a feature.

The same idea holds true for those who admire the glory of sunsets. Position outdoor eating or sitting areas so you can enjoy the evening hours without baking in the heat of summer, or create a trellis to shade you from the sun. A deciduous vine will provide lovely protection from the direct sun in summer, yet allow light to come through in wintertime, when it is much more welcome.

Even if you don't have a direct view of the sunrise or sunset, consider orienting your garden to the various times of day or evening, or even a city's lights at night, if that is what you enjoy.

Peace, light, calmness, an attitude of expansiveness towards all of life, a nurturing and giving nature— think about how you can bring that into your garden.

The Seasons

At mention of the different seasons, people usually respond with great enthusiasm. "Oh, I love daffodils in Spring! Springtime is my favorite time of year!" or "I love the fall colors, and drive around to see all the incredible trees! And I love the smell of walking through dry leaves, and the crispness in the air."

Of course, there are people who await the heat and sun, and days spent outdoors in summertime. Flowers stay in bloom for weeks, or months! Summer's luscious array of vegetables and fruits come into season. People can cook and eat outdoors, and spend more time out in their gardens.

And the cold, rainy, snowy, and cloudy days of winter bring a deeper appreciation for being inside, surrounded by the comforts of home. Winter is a more inward time. It allows people, and the garden, to rest and prepare for the warmer days ahead.

Every season has its beauties. But if one season is especially thrilling to you, then emphasize that time of year in your garden.

Spring

Spring symbolizes a happy time of new growth, new beginnings, and the promise of good things to come.

The cheerful yellow trumpets of daffodils are a classic herald of spring. Crocus, too, add early vibrant bursts of color.

Daffodils arrive in profusion from late winter to early springtime. They grow in various shadings of bright yellows, white, and orange, in shapes that can be fanciful, and color combinations that fascinate the eye.

Tulips are one of spring's treasures—with their elegant form and beautiful colors. I never tire of seeing them. From the time their young shoots poke up through the ground, I eagerly watch them grow taller, form leaves and buds, until finally... they open! Some even have a delicate fragrance that I rush outside to smell as soon as one opens, for it epitomizes spring for me.

Gardens come alive! New leaves unfurl into a bright spring green—a color seen only that brief moment each year. Flowering shrubs bloom in a multitude of colors. There is new growth everywhere! And it's time to plant seeds and seedlings in the warmer soil, so they can prosper and mature.

Summer

Summer is a time of abundance. There is more light, more warmth, more time that can be spent outdoors and in the garden, and more ways to enjoy being with family and friends. The abundance of warm days, fresh garden vegetables, ripe fruits, and months filled with flowers displaying their joyous colors, feels rich with life. Now is the time when the spirit of your garden can really shine!

As soon as the threat of frost is over in spring, the summer garden can begin to be planted. What do you look forward to most?

If you love gardening in summertime, a vegetable garden can be very fulfilling. The plants need thinning, weeding, watering, and harvesting—all kinds of loving attention can be lavished upon them. Once the soil starts to be warmed by the early summer sun, you can plant seeds outdoors, or young seedlings if you want a head start and earlier harvest. If you are new to vegetable gardening, then try to resist the temptation to plant lots of all your favorite vegetables—plus some you've never tried before. There is a limit to how many zucchini, or any vegetable, a person can eat!

Summer's annual show of color may be what you look forward to most. Nurseries are filled with flowers of every color! The annuals, newly planted each season, keep their colors all throughout the summer months. Most of these flowers are quite common, but add a happy familiarity to the garden. There are marigolds in yellows and oranges, petunias in a variety of bright colors, blue lobelia, the soft-petaled impatiens, and geraniums (Pelargoniums) in an assortment of bright reds, pinks, deep rose tones, oranges, and white.

Rose bushes burst with buds and blossoms opening in glorious displays. Colorful perennials like delphinium, dahlias, lilies, peonies, balloon flowers, asters, penstemon, and oriental poppies come back to life to create fabulous shows in your garden.

Whether you go all out for a garden filled with color, vegetables, and fruits, or simply want to liven up a few pots with your favorite summertime flowers, let your garden reflect the generous spirit of the season.

Autumn

The abundance of summer begins to slow down. The energy of the garden becomes more calm, with a spirit of change and reflection. If you are fortunate, your area experiences the glories of fall colors, with leaves magically transforming from quiet greens to multifarious hues of yellows, golds, oranges, crimsons, and rich deep reds.

Let your garden
reflect the
generous spirit
of the season.

Maples are perhaps most famous for their fall colors, and they deserve all the praise and admiration they receive. Even the so-called common variety of maple can be breathtaking in fall color. There are numerous varieties of maple that range from tall stately trees, to dwarf weeping forms. The different varieties specialize in particular fall colors: blazing reds, deep burgundies, soft yellows splashed with crimson, and nearly every autumn shade imaginable.

Yet many other types of trees contribute glorious hues, giving a magnificent performance in the autumn landscape. Sumacs put on one of the greatest displays in the garden of my childhood. Aspen trees, with their white bark and slender limbs, are seen covering whole mountainsides in golden leafy splendor. Dogwood leaves transform from a soft green in summer to surprising blends of dusky rose. And I especially enjoy the persimmon tree, which along with fall color,

keeps its ripening orange fruit hanging on the bare branches of the tree into early winter.

There are also shrubs and flowers that come into bloom during this time of year. Although not as grand as a 50-foot tree going through its transformation, flowers add a personal feeling and contribute considerably to the fall garden.

Chrysanthemums, or "mums" are one of the leading selections. It seems as though these flowers, that come in assorted shapes, are available in a wider choice of colors every year. Sometimes it's fun to co-ordinate the colors of Chrysanthemums with nearby trees that produce fall color. You can plant mums in either a complementary or contrasting hue, which adds a nice little surprise.

Where you live, you may discover many types of flowers that come into bloom in the fall, and some summer flowers that will carry on through

autumn. In seasonal gardens, this is your last hurrah before winter, so enjoy every bit of color you want!

Winter

Winter is a more quiet and introspective time. The sky is a paler blue, the days are shorter, and less time is spent out in the garden—if any time at all. In most areas, Nature uses this season to rest.

The focus shifts to the design of the landscape, the structures, and foundation plantings. The color and texture of bark, the shape of branches, and the form of trees and shrubs take on new importance. Deep greens look restful and saturated with color against a wintry sky—while bright reds are a bold contrast to the subdued background.

Shrubs with bright red berries are cheering with their tiny dots of color. Red flowers, too, brighten the landscape. In our climate, early camellias come into full bloom in the middle of winter. If your winter temperatures do not drop much below freezing, then cheerful pansies may do well filling pots or flowerbeds in your garden. Primroses, too, have a charming shape and presence, and come in a lively choice of colors.

If the winter months feel dreary to you, and flowers can't handle the cold in your garden, then bring blooms indoors to brighten your spirits. Cyclamen and the "Christmas cactus" are popular wintertime plants that may do well in your home. You can buy fresh flowers, too, as a reminder of your garden in bloom. Or dress up the garden with strings of lights on a tree, arbor, walkway, or special place you can see from a window. The festive lighting will give you a friendly greeting in every kind of weather.

No matter which time of year is your favorite, plan your landscape to have *some* color or interest during every season. Then your garden will remain an inspiration all throughout the year.

Creating and Building a Garden

Allow the garden to develop and unfold naturally, as it is being created. Mapping out a garden, and sticking exactly to the original plan, plant by plant, flower by flower, lights here, bench there, never works as well as allowing some freedom for the design to take shape as you go along. There will be shining moments of discovery, when you realize something you couldn't possibly foresee. As you infuse the landscape with your energy and sense of style, your garden will take on its own life and personality.

Techniques are vital to a beautifully executed landscape design—however, no matter how skilled, techniques alone will not give you an *inspiring* design. *Inspiration* is more important than technique. Always ask yourself, "What's trying to happen here?" Walk all around your garden. Where do you want to look to see something beautiful, colorful, or especially inviting? View the garden areas from different places, like the entryway to your garden, a deck, or the front door of the house. Look at the garden from inside the house, too. Walk past your property, or drive up to it to see what impression you get, and what you think needs changing or improving. Any new thoughts or ideas?

A garden is never completely done, with nothing left to change as the seasons and years go by. Try to look at your landscape with a fresh outlook each season, to keep your inspiration alive and involved in the garden.

Start working with an area you *are* sure of, laying it out, planting, adding finishing touches—whatever phase you are in. Often, you have to just go ahead and start in one area, even though you are not clear about what to do in all the rest. Once you know what seems right in one place, then be patient—what to do in the other places will become clear to you in time. Patience is necessary when working with Nature and her rhythms. Allow the landscape to evolve naturally, rather than try to force something to happen. Always remember to work *with* the energy of the garden.

Let everyone who shares your home have some feature in the garden that is particularly for them. Maybe you are the one with the main interest in gardening, but discover some way to include each individual. Find out what flowers, trees, or colors they would like to see. If plants do not spark their interest, then ask about bird feeders, wind chimes, a swing, a nice place to sit, or other outdoor features. Create spaces and features so everyone feels a special connection with their surroundings.

Entryways—Where the Garden Begins

The entryway to your house begins where people first approach your home. It may be just a few feet off the street, or far from the front door at a gated entry, but people can feel your greeting by the setting around the front walkway—before they reach the front door and enter your home. It is nice to establish a sense of visual welcome, and make the short journey to the doorway a pleasant one.

What characteristics or qualities do you want the main entrance to convey? Do you want a formal or informal place of entry? Do you want a tranquil approach, or a lively welcoming; a cozy-feeling place, or one with interesting features? Envision the appearance and feeling you want to give, as well as what *you* would like to experience upon coming home.

It's nice to give everyone something welcoming to see that conveys your personal touch—a pot of flowers by the door; a landscape that evokes a particular feeling; your favorite flowers, trees, shrubs, or vines planted along the walkway or at the entrance to the house; lights that you enjoy— or anything that makes you feel happy to be home. What brings you joy to see when arriving home is your way of greeting others, too.

Think about the texture and experience of the plants along walkways. Plants with large thorns or prickly leaves are obviously less friendly in close quarters. Yet the scent of roses is so alluring, you may want to include them, choosing fragrant varieties with smaller thorns to place along a path. Roses can also be planted behind a low-growing hedge that you can reach across to smell their blooms.

Some plants invite being touched for their scent or texture. Scented shrubs, vines, and flowers are nice to have near enough to a walkway that you can stop for a moment as you go by, and inhale deeply their sweet fragrances.

Many types of herbs will impart their scent when gently stroked, and can be engaging when tucked into rockeries, trailed over retaining walls, or planted in flowerbeds along an entryway. And the soft, furry texture of lamb's ears are a treat for children (and adults!) along a walkway where you can be stroke them for their endearing softness as you pass by.

The Physical Comforts

It's always nice to have a comfortable place to pause before entering the home. A covered area at your front door and other entrances will provide a protected place to stand out of the blazing sun or inclement weather. If you are building a new home, or remodeling, you may want to specify this in your design.

Also, provide yourself and others with enough lighting to see well along the entire length of your main walkways, especially on a dark, rainy night. This adds to the feeling that a warm welcome is awaiting you just ahead.

Your Personal Entrance and Walkways

Guests may use one entry, and you another. Is the entryway you use a pleasant one? If not, how can you make it nicer? Add something special that makes you smile or feel welcome where you enter your yard, even if your entrance is the driveway up to a garage. Maybe it's a beautiful tree that visually greets you, or favorite flowers or shrubs. A garage can be given a personalized touch with plantings, a decorative item, and a splash of color.

Private Places

A private place. I think every garden should have a place that is special and quite personal. Many times a garden is geared towards family activities, or designed for entertaining, or to look attractive. Yet, a private place to sit, work in the garden, or to see from the house, is very fulfilling.

Have a place that uplifts your spirits where *you* like to be outdoors, or can see from the house. A private place to sit, relax, gather herbs or work in the garden—we all need places where we can refresh our energies. The garden is a perfect place.

Scent

Gardenias, jasmine, roses, hyacinths, Oriental lilies, sweet-smelling violets, and other fragrant flowers are especially nice near entryways, along walkways, or underneath windows where their fragrance can float into the home through an open door or window. Scented geraniums, rosemary, and lavender are delightful along a walkway, too, where the branches reach up near hand level,

and can be touched while passing by, leaving their perfumed scent on your hand. And there are numerous aromatic groundcovers, like the tiny-leafed Corsica mint, which releases its minty scent into the air when touched by foot or fingertips.

The fragrance of some flowers is stronger in the evening. These blooms, such as jasmine and honeysuckle, are marvelous near a bedroom window, where their scent can waft into the room at night as you drift off to sleep.

Star jasmine, which is lovely year round, is beautiful climbing against a house, along a fence, or even grown as a groundcover, where its evergreen foliage is a boon when the vine is not blooming.

Scented vines or flowers are enticing near a front gate or entryway to your garden, where people strolling by can enjoy the sweet fragrance, and friends coming to your home will be greeted by the delicate perfume on their way to your door.

Visual Mystery

Create scenes of visual mystery, enticement, and wonder. Allow for the small delights of discovery.

Create a subtle lure with a curving path, or a walkway that turns a corner, while offering visual pleasures along the way. When the destination is hinted at, but not seen, it sparks curiosity, awakens interest, and causes one to wonder, "What's down this pathway? What does it look like over there? I wonder what's around that corner?" This is one appeal of a garden that makes it so pleasing to walk from one place to another.

How can you incorporate mystery and points of discovery into your garden and around your home? Gardens are like multi-dimensional paintings. The delight of a garden is that you can see a tantalizing hint of a wondrous thing, then move into the "painting" to experience the secret wonder.

What situations and images come to mind?

—For a place to dine out-of-doors: A glimpse of a charming table and chairs half-veiled by shrubs and flowers, or a decorative screen.

—A walkway goes along the side of your house, then turns a corner where you behold…? Make it special.

—The curving garden path, lined with sweet-smelling violets and flowering shrubs, leads gently towards…? A quiet place you want to go.

What would you find inviting? Have at least one area of mystery in your garden that suggests some special place lies just ahead especially when it leads to your front door.

Fences, Walls, and Garden Gates

A wall or fence may be designed for privacy, security, or protection from animals that enjoy feasting in your garden. Yet this same wall or fence can also create an intriguing sense of mystery and wonder. What *is* on the other side? Can you catch a glimpse as you go by? Do you see treetops, scenes of color and greenery through openings, or the entryway to the home through a gate?

To make a fenced or walled garden a friendlier place, add plantings *outside* the barrier, or allow for passersby to see parts of the garden over or through the screening. Think of what might be attractive or pleasurable for people passing by, and also form a nice greeting to those walking through the garden gate. Tall flowering trees or trees with vibrant seasonal color, scented vines, shrubs and flowers, an archway over the entry, or decorative feature to the gate are all welcoming choices.

SEVEN

Colors and Your Environment

Color has a tremendous effect on how we feel. Some colors give us energy, others are calming. We can resonate with certain hues more than others. What is cheerful to one person may be strident to another. What colors do *you* enjoy? How do they make you feel?

Soft, delicately colored blossoms; rich tones of lavender-through-violet; yellows; golds; oranges; innumerable shades of pink, rose, and red; light-to-darkest blues; deep purples; purest white; exotic blooms in uninhibited colors; the occasional glimpse of black; browns of bark and stem; and luxuriant greens everywhere. What choices there are!

Leaf and stem hues also should be looked at with a discriminating eye. There are silvery greys, deep plum tones, yellow-greens, blue-greens, grey-greens, and variegated greens with tints of rose, yellow, or white.

What colors will make you happy when you see them? What colors remind you of somewhere special, or a place you would like to visit on vacation? The blue shades may remind you of clear skies and water; yellows of sunny days; reds and oranges of tropical regions; greens of woodlands; and white blossoms of crystalline snow on mountain peaks.

Are there colors that will enhance or be an exciting accent for the colors of your house? Or do some colors conflict with the walls and cause a sense of discord? That's the last thing you want!

Here are some of my thoughts and observations: First, I love all colors. I do use some, like orange, more sparingly. I find orange very activating, so I use it only where I want that kind of mood or energy. Pinks are just pretty to me. Reds are eye-catchers. Yellows look cheerful and sunny. I am especially fond of the various rich blues and purples—very dignified and elegant. I always like some white, as an accent or restful feature. Deep violet and rosy blooms have an uplifting beauty to my eyes. And green. Green feels very nurturing and healing. I must have lots of greenery around me.

So, what are your thoughts? Make some notes to help you remember what to look for, or to avoid, when you shop for plants.

Some people NEED lots of color. Life to them looks too dull in quiescent environs. To feel refreshed and rejuvenated may require the use of striking combinations and bold primary colors. Reds, yellows, and oranges will grab attention.

Use them in combination with their opposite color on the color wheel to make the most vibrant statement. For contrast, put yellow with purple, red with green or white, and orange with blue. Reds are the most highly visible color in the garden (because of all the green foliage), and will lead the eye from place to place better than any other. Experiment with adding in other colors to give the total effect you want. Remember, though, in keeping with the concept of creating a garden that reflects who you are yet adds harmony and inspiration to your life, bring in elements that soothe and balance your spirit, not just add more energy. Be sure to have places of visual rest along with the vibrant colors.

Other people seek soft tones to bring more harmony into their lives. A mixture of gentle pinks and reds, shades of lavender, cheerful yellows, pure whites, and calming greens can encourage the feminine qualities of the heart—kindness, tenderness, compassion, and love.

To people who like a feminine (or even frilly) look, pinks in various shades, heights, and sizes are a must. White will be a lovely accent. But the delicacy of all pink or pink-and-white can become a bit much. Again, following the practice of bringing balance to one's life, add accents of blue and purple to the very "feminine garden" for some beneficial strength.

White is significant, as it emanates a sense of peace or purity, and offers a resting place for the eye in a garden punctuated with color. White reflects the luminescent glow of moonlight (or lamplight), and is the only color that stands out in darkness. All other blooms lose their beauty at night, fading into grey monochrome tones. Some people establish white as the theme to fill their entire gardens, calling them "moon gardens," using accents of white-blooming flowers, trees with white trunks, and shrubs with green-and-white foliage for a quiet and restful effect.

If a display of flowers will be seen from a distance, then use higher contrast and drama for the effect to remain vibrant from afar. Pale colors will be barely noticeable. Although yellow and purple are ordinarily quite bold, from a distance you may even want to add red, or another strong color, to help the combination really stand out. White accents will also act as a spotlight to feature the bold colors.

Color in the garden is treated the same way an artist adds color to a painting. Splashes of color may draw the eye to a doorway, perhaps, or highlight certain parts of the garden. Many people enjoy variety, using splashes of bold colors, quieter spots of leafy greens, areas with gentle pinks and violets, or a medley of colors scattered throughout. What I love about gardens is that you can change the colors of this art form from year to year, in whatever direction feels inspiring.

Color Tips and Planting Guide

When should you plant one color alone; two colors together; or three or more together? How do you know what to do? Use the following guideline for ideas, or as a reference when planting a single flowerbed, pots or urns, or flowerboxes. There are no absolute rules here!

When is it good to use a single block of color? What does it do?

One color planted on its own lets you fully appreciate the *visual beauty and feeling* of the color. If you like the *feeling* a certain color gives, such as cheerfulness with yellow, gentleness with pink, energy with red, or purity with white, then you will be able to experience it better if it is planted on its own. The *overall shape* of an area planted all in one color will also stand out more clearly.

What about using just two colors of flowers?

In art or design, using *even* numbers of items (colors in groups of 2, 4, 6, etc.) can look predictable and stiff; whereas *odd* numbers (1, 3, 5, etc.) create a pattern with an asymmetrical look and may be considered more harmonious and interesting. However, there *are* times when mixing two colors together provides just the effect you want.

Situation #1: Mixing two colors of the *same type* of flower. When the height, size, and shape is the same, the tendency is for the eye to bounce back and forth between the two colors—never quite able to rest or linger on either one. This friendly vying for attention produces an animated or lively look, as though the flowers are saying "Look at me! Look at me!" This may be exactly the effect you wish in order to wake up your energy when looking out a window, or to perk up a dull corner of the garden. The dance of color in the two-toned scheme creates a fun, bouncy, lively ambience that may mirror your own personality. A children's garden or play area is another prime location for a two-color combination, where a playful, animated look will add to the happy feeling.

The dance of color in the two-toned scheme creates a fun, bouncy, lively ambience that may mirror your own personality.

The outcome will be more dramatic if you are mixing two high contrast colors, such as red and white or yellow and purple, versus two colors that are closer in hue, such as two shades of pink. Some of the color-traits are: Yellow mixed with purple or blue is bright, cheerful, and awakening. Pink and white is sweet, happy, and feminine. Red and white is dramatic and spirited. Also, the flowers' foliage sometimes adds a neutral color to the total look, mellowing the contrast between the two colors.

Normally, it is best to match the mood of the plantings to the mood of the garden (or particular section of garden). In one instance I *did* successfully combine bold red and white flowers in a setting that looked more like a serene wood-land than a dramatic garden—but I had to work at it to get the two seemingly disparate energies to connect together. Instead of alternating red and white in a predictable order, I grouped an *odd* number of reds (3-5 plants), and planted them in an irregular or sweeping pattern. Then I planted an *odd* number of whites (5-7 plants), in an irregular sweep. I continually changed the number of plants of each color and the sweeping shapes of the planting pattern. The total effect was lovely. The tranquil garden was harmoniously enlivened by the colors, because the planting was done in a relaxed pattern that didn't allow the eye to bounce from one color to the other. The two dramatic colors flowed together in a natural interplay, adding their vibrant tones to the natural setting.

Situation #2: Underplanting: Mixing two colors with *different types* of flowers of *differing heights.* Underplanting gives a luxuriant feeling of depth and abundance. One type of flower alone could suffice, yet here there are *two* layers of blooms in lavish complement to one another. When underplanting, select a lower-growing flower to cover and fill the flowerbed with its color; then use another type of flower that grows taller, which can be dotted evenly throughout or clustered. Usually, the blossoms of the lower flowers are smaller in size than the taller blooms.

One of my springtime favorites is tulips underplanted with forget-me-nots or pansies. The tall, elegant tulips, all in one color, and the low-growing flowers underneath in another color, allow the beauty of each to stand out. You can use high contrast colors, like red tulips with a mass of white pansies underneath. Or plant softer blends such as peach tulips underplanted with the tiny sky-blue blossoms of forget-me-nots. Because the colors are seen one above the other, and the blooms are

of very different sizes, they are both featured at their best. Each color is clearly noticed, as when a single color is planted—only this way it looks more interesting. The effect is enchanting.

Another fabulous combination for tiered colors, this time using a summertime shrub with bedding plants, is underplanting hydrangea with impatiens. The blossoms of the impatiens nearly match the shape of the hydrangea's flower petals —except the hydrangea blooms are huge clusters of the petals compared to the single blossoms on impatiens. The petals' similarity in shape creates a natural connection between the two plants. What makes this especially compatible is that, as the intensity of color in the hydrangea's blossoms fade through the summer, one's attention drifts more to the lower color, and remains captivated by the beauty of the impatiens that still shows off the shape and subtler shades of the large blooms overhead.

You can plant multi-color mixes of impatiens under the hydrangea, or select single colors as an accent. Plan the color scheme around the

Underplanting gives a luxuriant feeling of depth and abundance.

hydrangea color (which may vary from year to year, depending upon soil conditions). If your hydrangea is pink, do you want to dress it up with a variety of colors underneath? Or would you rather have a more "proper" look with a white blanketing below? Do you like a blending of hues, where violet impatiens or one of the pale blush or soft pinks would be nice? For blue hydrangea, I like to customize a mix using three colors of impatiens, or single out one favorite.

I especially like some violet used in a blend. White impatiens alone, or in a mix, will make a restful balance. There are many colors to choose from that you might find charming. If you have one of the glorious white hydrangeas, let it glow in all its glory, with the color of impatiens in pleasing harmony. The red impatiens, though, seem a bit strong against the gentler "personality" of any hydrangea—at least in my surroundings.

Situation #3: Interplanting: Planting two *different types* of flowers, with *similar heights.* When two colors look fabulous together they can bring out the best in one another—the perfect partnership! I have favorite pairings I repeat from one

year to the next—although I may change the flowerbeds in which they are placed for variety. Two outstanding, widely available summertime choices are yellow marigolds with blue salvia; and red geraniums (Pelargonium) with blue or purple salvia. The more slender stems of the salvia with the spire shape of the blooms makes for a nice counterpoint to the larger, rounded blossoms of marigolds or geraniums. Red salvia is also used to interplant, although personally, I favor the blue. To interplant, you can plant the two types of flowers either fully integrated, with the salvia interspersed evenly throughout, or you can use less of the salvia, so that it becomes an occasional accent. The opposing shapes of slender spires and round flowerheads creates a cozy, nestled-in-together look.

When do three colors, or more, work best? How do you know which colors to combine? Do you need to be an artist to get it right?

Three colors, or more, of the *same type* of flower: A mixture of colors produces an overall impression. The more colors that are mixed, the more each individual hue tends to merge with the others, rather than flaunt its own beauty. The experience is usually the general mood of the blend. If you mix purple, orange, and pink, the effect will be more daring than if you combine violet, pink, and white. Do you want a "Wake up!" mood, or a soothing symphony of color? Are there other colors in adjacent flowerbeds that will intensify or mellow out the theme?

Customize your own blends by playing with different color combinations at the nursery, to see what you like and the feeling it gives you. Or, if you are choosing flowers that come in a wide variety of colors, like petunias and impatiens, you will them also sold in established mixes. Then you don't have to decide exactly what colors to com-

bine—you get them all! There may be more of one color or another, but will that matter to you?

Three colors, or more, of *different types and heights* of flowers: Deep flowerbeds, flower-boxes, and pots or tubs of flowers often belong in this category. The cascading interplay of color adds drama, a sense of movement, and a feeling of completeness. In flowerbeds, the taller flowers are able to visually connect with the ground via the descending layers of color. In containers, the colors tumble down to the edge or trail over as though reaching for the ground. You can use commonplace flowers to great effect, or bring in exotic blooms as a prominent feature.

For an easy summer layout in a sunny flowerbed, you may like to interplant yellow marigolds with blue or purple salvia, then add a cheerful border of purple-with-white petunias along with some tinier bright blue lobelia. In this instance, the simple yellow and blue-to-purple theme is repeated in a charming way.

Always ask yourself what kind of feeling you want to create. Do you want a gentle blend in relaxing hues? A bold statement of color? A little brightness amongst other colors? Do you want a bit of surprise with vegetables or fruit mingling with your flowers? Keep in mind what you want to experience, then choose colors to support the theme.

Nurseries are good places to experiment with combinations, as various types of flowers may already be in full bloom and you can see how you like them together. Hold colors together to see if you like their blend or amount of contrast. If the flowers will be planted by shrubs or at the base of a tree, take a sampling of flowers near a similar shrub or tree in the nursery to see if the colors and foliage are nice accents for one another. That way, you will have an idea of what works, and what doesn't, in your situation.

In nature, there are subtleties and blends of color unimaginable in other forms of art. See what works in your own garden, your setting, your life. You are not working with paints or fabric, but with living colors! Whichever colors you choose, in whatever style or mix of plantings, use what makes you feel your best. Experiment. Discover what enriches you, and inspires the feelings you want in your garden: joy, harmony, inner peace, light, an expansive view of life, love, and respect for all creation.

In nature,
there are subtleties
and blends of
color unimaginable
in other forms
of art.

EIGHT

Repetition

Visual connections through repetition will give your garden a feeling of wholeness, completion, and harmony. The connections can be made using color, shapes, textures—or a combination of these elements.

Repeat one or more colors throughout the garden to draw the eye from one spot to another, draw attention to points of interest, and establish focal points. Experiment with the number of places you would like the repetition—the goal is to lead the eye through the garden in a pleasing way, without feeling bombarded by the overabundance of a color. If you are working with several colors in your repetition, you may want to single out one of them to be the primary leader, with the other colors repeated a little less often. The color scheme of the house can be a part of the repetition, too.

Shapes are a major part of every landscape design. A natural looking landscape will have

gently curving lines in pathways, flowerbeds, open areas, and terracing. In nature, plants also grow with a softness or flow to their arrangement, with clusters of plants that are particular to that location growing together in informal groupings.

For this natural look, select plants that you would like to see in more than one location in your garden. Use them like a theme, that recurs in slightly different formations throughout your landscape. Include several *different* types of plants in separate groupings to make your design more interesting. For example, plant roses along entryways, rhododendrons and azaleas beneath large shade trees, and Japanese

maples as ornamental trees. You may have a large landscape where you can have totally separate types of gardens, but in most instances it is nice to have a recurring theme to give a garden continuity and a sense of harmony.

Identifiable shapes in your garden will make a stronger statement. Circular, rectangular, square, triangular, star, and other shapes can be repeated either in the design layout of walkways and flowerbeds, or in shaping the shrubbery into decorative forms and formations.

Repetition and continuity through texture allows you a great deal of leeway. Everything has texture! For example, you can use rock as a theme—with rock walls, large boulders, rocks that are a feature of your walkways and patios, or rocks used in more than one design feature. Foliage, too, can be the way you visually tie the garden together, using similar shrubs, trees, or flowers repeated throughout your overall design.

You may decide to use a blending of several elements to link the landscape together—rock walls, shrubbery with similar leaf-shapes as a backdrop, and your favorite color of flowers to lead the eye through the landscape picture.

If your garden is large enough that you have completely separate areas that will not be seen together, you *can* have different styles in the different spaces. Yet the concept of repetition holds true for each area that is visually connected, or that you wish to connect with a similar look or feeling.

Whichever way you incorporate repetition as a visual guide, the overall effect should create a visual connection that unites your landscape, and remains enticing. You want just enough that it sparks the imagination, and lures you to want to see more.

NINE

Vignettes from Your Windows

The pathways leading to your house, and vignettes from the windows, are areas that will bring you pleasure every day if landscaped attractively.

Captivating vignettes of the garden, seen through the windows and doorways of the house, are one of the most frequent experiences you'll have of your garden. Such a view should trigger the thought of how attractive or inviting it is, and how much you would enjoy being there.

In our home, we enjoy spending most of our time in the kitchen, so our garden is more intensively landscaped outside the kitchen windows and the doorway that opens onto a patio. While doing dishes, we look upon tiered flowerbeds and calming, green shrubbery. From the breakfast nook, where I also write, we enjoy a view of our shade garden, and a small waterfall with a

table and chairs just visible in their own alcove. I like being able to see the outdoor dining area from the kitchen, where its lure beckons with the recurring thought, "It looks so inviting—wouldn't it be nice to eat there!" In our anticipation, we begin enjoying the meal even before we are seated outside. Just looking at the space is enticing.

Most people spend more time looking out at their gardens than they spend outdoors, so it's worthwhile creating alluring scenes from these indoor perspectives.

Which rooms that have views of the outdoors do you spend the most time in? Your kitchen? An office? The bedroom? A living,

dining, or sitting room? How would you like to enhance those spaces?

You can add outdoor features that have a personal appeal, and display one of your interests. Or you can

create a setting that brings you a particular feeling—of calmness, relaxation, happiness, inspiration, or whatever relates best to you and that room. For instance, outside a bedroom window, you may want to see flowers in colors that help you to feel perkier in the morning, and encourage a cheerful outlook to start your day.

Vignettes can also have a significance. Outside a kitchen window, you can incorporate features that relate to cooking—an herb or vegetable garden, fruit trees, or a place to cook or dine outdoors—as the garden's extension of the kitchen theme. If your house has a definite architectural style, such as French provincial, then you can extend the theme even further with plantings outside your kitchen window that remind you of a French landscape—

like borders of lavender, rosemary and other herbs used in French cuisine, olive trees, or grape vines. This expands the feeling of the kitchen out into the garden, and gives a purpose behind the selection of plantings you choose, linking everything together.

The outside colors and shapes can be an extension of the design in your room. Pick out colors that are on your walls, upholstery, rugs, draperies, or furnishings, and extend them outdoors in the colors of flowers and foliage. In one friend's house, she has a luscious red wall in her living room with large windows that look upon an inner courtyard. She picks up the colors of her red wall and living room accents by including flowers in complementary shades of red amongst the plantings. Her courtyard looks and feels like an enchanting part of the living room.

When treating the outdoors as an extension of the interior space, you can select colors that

harmonize, or work as a contrast to the interior hues, depending upon the effect you wish.

Shapes can also extend from one space to another. If your furnishings are modern and angular, you can incorporate angular art, pathway or patio materials, or garden furniture to extend your choice of interior design into the garden. Or if your furniture is soft and cushiony with rounded edges, then you may like your plantings, paths, and outdoor furniture to have curving or rounded lines, and a soft, layered look, qualities that make your view into the garden seem a natural extension of the house's interior.

A vignette may also be designed like a painting —meant to be admired for the way it looks, and the feelings it evokes. A garden bench may be set, picturesquely, under an arbor, along a path, or under a tree for its visual pleasure, rather than as a location people will regularly sit to rest. Seeing a place of repose creates an atmosphere of relaxation, and the thought of a restful time when one can sit quietly and simply admire the garden. A priceless image! Viewing this type of setting from the house, one's imagination sparks the sensation of already being there.

Remember to design your landscape so it is attractive from every perspective—including the vignettes from your windows!

TEN

Reflections

Still water reflects the sky above, and nearby plantings. What do you wish to see mirrored on the surface of the water—a soothing picture, or gaily colored images?

For pools or ponds in *natural* settings, reproduce scenes that you might see in nature: soft green reflections of leaf and frond; slender, arching branches overhanging the water's edge; blossoms on trees and shrubs echoed in watery images; the timeless presence of moss-covered rocks; upright grassy stems; and trailing tendrils reaching for moisture.

A stylized reflecting pool or swimming pool has a different spirit, and is often surrounded by more colorful plantings. The twin image of flowers appears real in a pool's reflection. Statuary takes on additional life with a dual form. Lights become more enchanting when reflected on the glistening surface. And every day one sees ephemeral scenes of the sky, with passing clouds, the colors of sunrise and sunset, and shadows from changing weather. These fleeting perceptions bring a magical world to what is simply—a pool of still water.

Look for these reflections when landscaping around water, and place your plantings and other features accordingly, for the best viewing.

There are other ways to reflect scenes in nature. Mirrors inside the house can bring garden images into a room, reflecting the outdoor colors like an ever-changing painting on the wall. Flowers in a

hanging basket outside a window can be mirrored into a room, to bring their color inside. You no longer have to look directly out the window to see the blooms, they appear in two places now! Position your mirror on the wall opposite what you wish to see when you are in the room, or walking by.

Mirrors can also be positioned to capture a distant vista or section of your garden, so it can be admired from more places in your home.

The polished surface of granite countertops also gives mirror-like reflections of color and images, seen against the beauty of the stone. Kitchens and bathrooms, especially, can employ this additional feature if reflective stone is part of the interior decor.

Reflections have their own mystery and excitement. Colors are seen where they don't really exist, and images are not where they seem to be. It's a delightful experience of the garden!

Colors are seen
where they
don't really exist,
and images are
not where they
seem to be.

ELEVEN

Enliven Your Garden

With All Kinds of Things!

Many people have told me they love their gardens but don't want to spend time working in them, or planting flowers every season. So, what adds life to a garden other than flowers? Bring in movement, color, a place for people

to be, garden art or statuary, and water—which can also draw birds, butterflies, and animals. Alternatives to flowers abound! There are things to see, places to be, and sounds to listen to.

Things to See

Bring color, movement, and art into your garden!

Items made of fabric make an animated contribution. A string of colorful flags can be tacked up along roof lines, or suspended above a walkway, patio, deck, or entryway where their occasional fluttering movements can be enjoyed. A windsock or windsleeve is especially fun for people who like to observe wind and weather condi-

tions. Hang a windsleeve at the corner of your house, or above a deck or patio—wherever it will have freedom of movement to lift and catch the winds coming from all directions.

One garden I visited had the delightfully creative accent of pink-purple-and-white beach umbrellas with their handles stuck in the ground. The umbrellas were shading pink-blooming hydrangeas that were getting too much mid-day sun. The colors of the umbrellas became part of a large garden-bouquet with pink hydrangeas and sprightly upright fuchsia-colored annuals. This whimsical touch showed the artistic and imaginative personality of the woman living

there—PLUS, they were a creative way to protect her plants until they could be moved to a better location the following year.

Movement

Twirling mobiles will add movement and decoration with colorful and artful shapes and designs. Place them in various spots around your garden, so you can see them from the house, or catch glimpses of their movement from walkways.

Art

Do you have an area in your garden, such as a blank wall or fence, an immovable slab of rock, or a drab empty space, that could use a prominent piece of art?

Artwork or sculpture can be anything from a serious piece of art to humorous pink flamingos. Would you like a decorative element in your garden to represent an interest you have, such as a love for wildlife, or appreciation for classical sculpture? Or would you prefer artwork that

reinforces a quality you wish to develop, such as a loving or joyful view of life, or a meditative nature? There are carvings of all sizes in wood and stone; artworks in copper, brass and other metals; and for inspirational art, statuary of saints and holy personages. Look around until you find what suits you and your garden perfectly!

Lighting

Lighting has a practical function in the garden —illuminating parking areas, walkways, decks and patios, and entryways to your home. There are a vast number of fixtures available for practical purposes, in a wide variety of styles.

Yet lights also create an atmosphere. Would you like the glow of candlelight in a dining area, the soft luminescence of a lantern along a walkway or set in a lush flowerbed, a string of cheerful lights above a patio? Select light fixtures that bring you enough light to see by and enhance the mood you wish to create, in styles that harmonize with the design of your home.

Are you also wishing for a magical evening scene to be a feature of your garden? Colored spotlights can accent specimen trees or areas of special interest. Place lights so the illumination will focus on the

form of a tree or a sculpture, cast its glow over a bed of flowers, or create the atmosphere you wish over a broader area.

The graceful form of a weeping Japanese maple, with its delicate leaves and branches touching the earth, can be serenely uplit with a soft red light to showcase the tree's exquisite beauty. Or a simple wall of green ivy may be beautifully spotlit with a mellow green light to create a relaxing glow for a backdrop.

Choose garden lighting that suits your nature and your setting. Will colored lights add to the effect you wish, or would you prefer a soft white luster? Look at the effect the lights have from various viewpoints—from the windows of your house, the garden, and the approach to your home.

You will be seeing them from all perspectives.

Places to Be

The garden is a fabulous place to relax, unwind, and enjoy life. In addition to the joys of gardening, there can be places to cook, dine, play, swim, relax in the fresh air, and enjoy a space created just the way you like it to be!

Outdoor Cooking, Dining, and Seating

I love to grill summertime meals out on our patio, and dine in a shady nook surrounded by flowers and trees. To me, that is the epitome of summer dining.

Cooking outdoors makes a meal feel special, like a small celebration. The food may be simple, or a grilled culinary extravaganza—either way, cooking outside lends a mystique to any meal.

It doesn't take much space to cook outdoors—just a place for a grill, and if you have room, a side table for holding utensils and the food destined for your table. When I was young, my father grilled out on the small back porch off our

kitchen, with great results. Nowadays, many people are so enchanted with outdoor cooking and grilling, they set up fully-equipped kitchens in their yard.

Even if you don't prepare your meal outside, dining in the fresh air of your own garden can be a delight. Would

along with practicality. In some instances, garden furniture looks like a work of art. The styling, materials the furniture is made of, number of pieces, and placement, contribute greatly to the appeal of your outdoor area. What will go with the looks and mood of your house and garden?

you like to sit outside in the early morning, for a mid-day luncheon, afternoon tea, or evening meal? The ambience of your dining spot is often more important than the size of the space. Give the seating arrangement your personal touch in the style and placement of table and chairs. Select furniture that is comfortable and easy to take care of, so you will enjoy using it. Also, incorporate any shade, screening, or other protection you may need during the time of day you wish to be in your special outdoor place.

Furniture

Outdoor furniture adds style and character

A small stylish pair of bistro chairs with round metal table establish a very different tone from cushioned armchairs around a large wooden table. Every style has its own charm. Think about what furniture shapes you would like that also complement the design of your house—square, rectangular, round, curving, or linear. What material fits in with your setting and climate conditions—metal, wood, wicker, marble or stone, or a composite material? What style characteristics will visually complement your garden—ornate or delicate, solid-looking and substantial in size, sleek, modern, old-fashioned, traditional or contemporary designs, formal or informal?

Do you want the furnishings to visually say "garden" or "living area" with their arrangement and setting? A bench amongst the trees and flowers feels a part of the garden, whereas a covered deck with a group of chairs that look soft and cushiony with colorful pillows feels like an outdoor

living room. Consider if you want the emphasis on the garden, on relaxation, or on entertaining. Maybe you have enough room to establish separate areas for different activities?

Outdoor furniture has several functions. The most obvious—you intend to use it! But that can be the least of its contributions. Its visual appeal acts as a lure that draws people outside, into that area of the garden. The type of furniture you choose also makes a statement about what you like to do outdoors. Do you have a place to dine, a hammock under the trees, loungers by a pool? Furniture also creates an impression about your home.

By our front door, we have two benches that are used only occasionally, but which visually create a welcoming feeling when approaching the house. Their silent message invites people to come, sit, and stay for a while. This visual greeting is just what I like at the entrance to our home. Even though two benches are not necessary in a practical sense, I can't imagine the space without them.

A garden bench, a table and chairs, a hammock beneath the trees—who cares if they are frequently used when they contribute to the beauty and feeling you want in your garden!?

Time to Play

Do you have children, or like outdoor activities? Are there sports or games suited to your garden? My childhood neighborhood had places where my friends and I could play basketball, badminton, volleyball, and croquet, as well as skateboard, roller skate, jump on a trampoline,

Birdsong, the sound of running water, and the tinkling of bells and windchimes can soothe our nerves, help to clear our minds, and invite an inner peace.

and enjoy group games where we would run and hide. My favorite place of all was my best friend's treehouse. We had a grand time!

A treehouse, rope swing, playhouse, or backyard play equipment give children, and the young in spirit, a lighthearted place outdoors where they can sit, play, and have fun. One couple I know, who are in their 80s, continues to have tea together on the patio in front of a playhouse, even though their children are long since grown. When their children and grandchildren visit, everyone happily heads out to the back garden and gathers around the cheerful little house to have tea, cookies, and share in the small joys of life. Fun, laughter, and the feeling of freedom and enjoyment of each day is important at any age.

Let the Sounds in Your Garden Be a Balm to Your Spirit

Bring an aura of peace and the sounds of nature and inspiration into your garden. Create the haven you seek.

The sounds in our environs can have a deep and powerful effect on us. Birdsong, the sound of running water, and the tinkling of bells and windchimes can soothe our nerves, help to clear our minds, and invite an inner peace.

Bells

Church bells, temple bells, gongs, and chimes are heard throughout various cultures as a call to the heart and spirit of the people. In our home gardens, we can recreate this timeless experience.

The breath of Nature plays music through the ringing of windchimes and sprightly tinkle of wind bells in an ever-changing variation of melody. A slight breeze, and only a note or two may play. In a storm-driven wind, a great symphony is heard—dispelling the fierceness of the weather with the beauty of harmonious chiming. Nature always has her surprises. Some days her bell-tones may not be heard at all—then suddenly, a few ringing notes. Then quiet again. How delightfully capricious!

Windchimes and wind bells draw attention to an area with their music and ornamental charm. Where would you like these lovely instruments? They can be artfully positioned near the doorway to your home; under the eaves of rooftops or porches; fastened out on a balcony; or hung near a window so that they can be seen as well as heard.

Are there areas in your garden that could use enlivening? Dangle wind chimes from the branch

of a tree, or use a decorative hanger to attach them to a fence, trellis, or near a garden gate. Windchimes and bells can be set out in your garden like pieces of artwork, too, or you may like the bouquet-style garden bells.

I often like windchimes or bells by entrances to a home. Their visual charm and music creates a wonderful flow of energy. In our own garden, a windchime hangs within easy reach of our garden gate that we use every day. We are in the comfortable habit of lightly touching the wind-catcher to set the chimes ringing whenever we pass by. The lilting bell-tones travel softly into our home and through our garden in a friendly fashion, as though saying, "Hello! I'm home!" or "Good-bye for now!" every time we come or go.

Choose the location of your chimes or bells according to your wind conditions. If you live in a very windy location, you may want your chimes in a somewhat protected spot so you can enjoy their natural melody rather than a constant clamoring. However, if you have only occasional strong winds, then position your chimes where they can catch every breeze.

A gong adds an architectural detail that is befitting to an Asian-style house, garden, or outdoor meditation place. A gong's deep reverberations sound only when struck, so position a gong where it can be approached and rung, or else admired for its beautiful design and implied call to contemplation and meditation.

Water Sounds

Fountains, streams, and waterfalls provide movement, beauty, and the soothing sound of flowing water—each has its own unique sound and quality. The spray of a fountain can be gentle or exuberant, the current of a stream can be tranquil or tumbling, a waterfall may flow smoothly and serenely over the edge of a rock or fall rushing to a pool below.

Moving water revitalizes the air in its surroundings, and feels refreshing and soothing to our inner being. The sound of water also muffles less pleasing sounds.

These are welcome features near the entrance to a home, in a private courtyard or niche in a garden, and within sight and sound of an outdoor seating area.

How much water movement, and how much sound you want to listen to is very individual. Consider whether you want your environment to offer a sense of calm and healing, or be more refreshing and rejuvenating. The sound of rushing water creates a different atmosphere from that of a gentle flow.

Birdsong

Birdsong is a gift of nature. The birds' joyous songs of freedom voice a celebration of life. We are captivated by even their simplest notes, and their melodies and twitterings help uplift our thoughts.

Birds of all kinds will be drawn to your garden by the sound of water, from a small drip into a birdbath to the murmuring of a fountain or stream. Different types of seed, fruit, and berries attract specific species, but EVERY bird needs a drink of water.

For a simple set-up (available through wild bird stores), have water drip from overhead into a shallow birdbath. The drip should be elevated a foot or more above the birdbath, and drip every five seconds or so. The tiny drip of water makes the water move, which will attract more birds than a stagnant pool. Your garden will have the greatest variety of birdlife with this simple offering. Just give them a little time to discover the new source of refreshment.

If you also wish your birds to have a place to bathe, you will need to give them a little privacy and protection, along with a shallow spot for them to wade in "ankle deep" for their ablutions.

Birds are vulnerable when they bathe. As they dip their heads into the water and splash about, they are no longer able to keep a watchful eye against predators. Choose a bathing spot a little out of the way so they can sense it's their own space. Make sure cats cannot reach them without being seen, and hawks or other birds of prey are not able to easily swoop in upon them. Nearby trees or a trellis will give the little birds a place to escape to, if needed.

Do you want a lot of bird activity in your garden, or a more peaceful place? If your garden is a tranquil refuge for you, then just offer the birds some water—the birds will come and go fairly quietly. But if you like a lot of bird activity, and want to watch and listen to the lively flutterings and chattering while they feed, then set out bird feeders, too.

Make it Count

Whatever you add to your garden—colorful fabrics, mobiles, chimes or bells, artwork, a place to cook or dine, special lighting, furniture in a favorite style, a water feature, or enticements for wild birds—add in only one or two items at a time, then take a look to see if the space is improved. If the new selection does not *contribute* and make that part of your garden look and feel better, then try something else. Each time you add something to your garden, ask yourself—"Is my garden nicer now, or was it better before?"

TWELVE

The Practical Versus Your Dream

Maintaining Your Garden

My practical words of advice are to have a garden a size you are able to maintain. Did I do that? No. Do I wish I did? No. Nevertheless, it's good advice. It just depends on your nature. My garden, less than immaculately kept, is still a wonderful refuge for me. I prefer it when the flowerbeds are all weeded and filled with a joyful show of color, the lawn neatly mowed, the fruit trees pruned, the roses well tended, and everything fertilized on a regular schedule. But that is not my normal reality, and I still wouldn't give up any part of the garden.

But if having a showcase garden is part of your dream, then think seriously about how much you can honestly and realistically maintain, or hire others to maintain for you.

There are fabulous ways to fill a garden with shrubs, trees, and flowers that require a minimum amount of care compared to tending a vast vegetable garden, acreage of lawn, large numbers of roses, or other high-maintenance garden plants.

Constant weekly maintenance can turn into a bothersome chore over time. I love the lush, soothing green of lawns (and have one), but lawns in our climate need mowing at least once a week during their growing season, which is six to seven months of the year. That isn't so bad in early May, when the fresh scent of cut grass is a welcome herald of warm days ahead. But by the end of September, the weekly mowing, periodic fertilizing, and seasonal maintenance can lose its charm. Some days I look at our lawn and wonder how it can *possibly* need mowing once again.

One can silently grow in attunement with the life of the plants, the outdoor breezes and fragrances, and savor some quiet time with nature at the beginning of a new day.

Similarly, many people find hand watering plants to be a pleasing ritual that is quietly therapeutic. One can silently grow in attunement with the life of the plants, the outdoor breezes and fragrances, and savor some quiet time with nature at the beginning of a new day.

However, you may find hand-watering more of a daily discipline than pleasing routine. Consider what will work best for you and your size of garden. An irrigation system may be a worthwhile investment, even for a garden comprised of a few pots on a deck.

The Charm of Small Gardens

Small gardens have much to their advantage. They don't require much water, and usually can be cared for quite easily. Plus, their manageable size seems to encourage trying new things, and giving the garden a loving, personal touch. A small garden can be quite charming, with details no large garden can possibly include. For those who have larger landscapes, there may be some area of the garden that can be made smaller and more intimate. It may turn out to be your favorite place.

Types of gardens

If you like to do the same thing, about the same time, and keep to a regular schedule every day, then garden elements that require that kind of attention may be perfect for you. A lawn that needs regular mowing, and plants that need frequent pruning and feeding are more likely to please you, and will allow you to give plenty of loving energy to your garden. Roses and vegetable gardens are naturals for someone who wants to be very involved with gardening.

If, however, you squirm at the thought of a fixed daily or weekly routine, then a garden that is more flexible with its maintenance is probably better for you. Some types of trees, shrubs, and flowers have very few needs. You may want only perennial flowers (those that come back year after year), rather than annuals which need to be replaced in each blooming season.

If you love some of summer's annuals such as petunias, marigolds, impatiens, and begonias, then you can always put some in a small, manageable-sized flowerbed or in a few well-placed pots where you can enjoy their profusion of color and not feel burdened by a lot of replanting each year. You can hook up your pots to an irrigation system on a timer, and your flowers can grow to be lush and happy with minimal care.

THIRTEEN

The Spirit of Gardening

Gardens are ever-changing and growing. Nature doesn't stop for a moment. Year after year the garden won't be exactly the same. One year, the garden looks glorious with fresh growth and color. Another year, it is not quite at its peak because of early heat, or the bite of cold. Yet the spirit with which you create and tend your garden can continually grow throughout the years, into greater harmony, fulfillment, inspiration, and happiness.

A garden is a great teacher. We must learn to give love before we can receive it, experience harmony within ourselves before we can create it outwardly, develop inner qualities of peace, happiness, joy, contentment, and love before it can fully manifest outwardly in a garden. This is why creating and caring for a garden can be such a deeply inspiring experience.

A garden with spirit reflects a uniqueness of its own. Let your garden be a channel for your love, creativity, nurturing, kindness, thoughtfulness, attunement to Nature and the Divine behind all creation, and bring you to an ever-deepening respect and love for all life.

A garden, even a very simple one, can be a place of great inspiration—a beacon of light and beauty in the world.

FOURTEEN

Supplementary Guide

PRACTICAL TIPS FOR BUILDING YOUR GARDEN

Pointers for New Construction

Think about what you would like, and take future owners into account.

—Create a way to walk all around your house, with pathways, or easy-to-use access.

—Place *at least* one electrical outlet on each side of the house, or every 30 feet. Doorways are key places where you are likely to need power for walkway or patio lights, an irrigation timer, or occasional items like an electric starter for a charcoal grill. Another need for electricity is a pump for a fountain or pond, plus any lighting you want for them. If you plan to have a garden feature with running water, or outside lighting, you may want to install switches for them inside your home. The wiring should also be made easily accessible for future hook-up.

—Water spigots! Don't short yourself. It is no fun dragging around 100 feet of garden hose. Give yourself a hose bib near every doorway, and near where you will park a car. Also, make sure a garden hose can get water to anyplace around your house, even if you don't plan to use the entire area. It is much easier to install hose bibs during the initial construction than add them later on.

—Plan for the future. Water and electrical are essential for certain outdoor features: irrigation, decorative water elements, shed or project areas, outdoor lights, and a garage. Even if you think you won't want extra outdoor features, lifestyles change, and you or a future owner may want to add some later on.

It's easy to do what is called "stubbing out" for water and electrical when the foundation of the house is being formed. Incorporating stub-outs during initial construction can save a great deal of expense and hassle in the future.

If your house is being built on a slab: When the water supply line is brought to the house, add a "T" connector one foot or so before the line reaches the footing of the slab (or where the tee will be easily accessible). Cap off the end of the "T" designated for garden water. Then you can tap into the water line for garden use, when needed. Electrical is accessible through the wall of the house in this situation.

If your house is being built on foundation walls: When the forms are being built for the foundation walls, include a 2"–3" diameter ABS or PVC pipe through the forms, beneath the ground level, that will allow access from underneath the house out to the garden. Cap off the ends to keep out dirt and small animals. The plastic pipe gives you access through the concrete foundation, allowing you to run water and/or electrical lines to the outside. Otherwise, if you want extra water or power lines run out to your garden, you will need to cut a hole throught the concrete foundation wall, which is a *much* bigger job and expense. You may also put a tee in the main water line to the house, as when building on a slab.

Also, before you build walkways, especially next to your house, lay a piece of 2"–3" diameter ABS or PVC pipe beneath the walkway—like an underground tunnel—to allow passage for irrigation or electrical lines from one side of the walkway to the other. Cap off the open ends of the pipe until you are ready to run your water or electrical lines. Garden walls are another area to place the ABS or PVC pipe, for access underneath to the outside of the wall.

Take photos of what you do! It's very easy to forget exactly where things are placed undergound. You may think you'll remember, but it is surprisingly easy to forget this kind of detail. A picture can save a lot of time.

—Drainage. Don't neglect it. We were assured by our architect that we wouldn't have problems with water along the front of our home, which is set several feet lower than the front garden. I was new to the world of landscaping, and believed him. That first winter we had to wade through water over a foot deep that had pooled all along the front of our home. Fortunately it didn't come under the front door. We then had to hand-dig a 150-foot trench to install a drainage system after the house was built and all the machinery was gone. Plan ahead. Remember that water always flows downhill. If your garden is higher than your home, OR your neighbors' land is higher, then expect to put in good drainage to protect

your home from flooding during heavy rains or snow-melts, and channel water away from the foundation of the house. It's a wise place to invest your money.

—Porches or a covered space over a door. Protect yourself and other people who come to your home. No one wants to stand in the rain, snow, or summer sun at the entrance to a house. Provide cover and a place people can pause and anticipate a welcome step into the home. The extra roof will also protect the doorways from heavy rains.

Construction and Design Tips for Walkways and Paths

Consider the function of the pathway—is it a main entry, quiet garden path, or a well-used walkway to a play area, pool, garage, shed, or greenhouse?

Think about how wide you would like the walkway. If you want two people to be able to walk comfortably side by side, then I suggest a walk to be 5 feet wide. If walking single file is fine with you, and a narrower walkway will look good with the house, then 3 1/2 feet is a comfortable width. For narrower garden paths in more personal sections of the garden, a 2 1/2-foot width works well, as long as the plantings alongside the path will remain fairly low to the ground. You may feel crowded brushing against shrubbery.

Will you be rolling a wheelbarrow along the path for garden clean-up or composting? Then make sure it is wide enough, and flat enough, for you to manage the wheelbarrow comfortably and to make any turns. Get out your wheelbarrow and make some runs back and forth, to see what is EASY for you to manage. There is no point in struggling along—you won't like using the wheelbarrow if it is always a challenge.

Also, choose path materials that suit your needs. Brick, stone, concrete, gravel, wood, crushed shells, or bark all have their pluses and minuses. Select which works well for you, gives you the traction you need in wet conditions, and harmonizes with your garden environment.

Once your walkways are established, make sure they are well lit for night-time travel, and make the journey pleasurable with attractive plantings or other features.

Creating a Layout for Walkways and Paths

If you are creating new paths, then spend time walking the land. Go back and forth over an area *many* times. I avoid looking down at the ground, unless I need to for safety. Try to look ahead, where you want to go. Once there, turn around and head back. Is the route the same, or slightly different? Pay attention to where you would like to go, and note if there is an obstruction in your way that can be moved.

Take the time to be sensitive to your surroundings. Is there a flowerbed that gets trampled, a spot where you would rather take a more direct route? Then, if you can, change the pathways to coincide with where people *like* to walk. Sometimes the natural flow is close to the house, whereas other times it's more natural to walk a little farther away. Try to look at the space as though there were nothing there. Walk back and forth. It will probably be very close to the same spot going both directions. Once you establish approximately where the pathway should go, then it's time to mark the boundaries or edges.

I use agricultural lime or white flour from the kitchen to mark the ground, but any light-colored powdery product that won't harm the soil or plants can be used. Put some of the marking substance in a container that you can easily dip your hand into, or that has a pour-spout for sprinkling directly onto the ground. I like to handle the marking powder and sprinkle it with my hand, but you may prefer shaking it out directly from the container.

To establish the borders or edges of the pathway, walk along keeping your arm down at your side and a little away from your body. Sprinkle some of the powder onto the ground as you walk. Be sure you don't look down and "decide" where the powder should go—just walk naturally and face straight ahead, and go where it feels right to walk. You'll be marking out your pathway area numerous times, so don't worry about getting the lines exactly right the first time.

Once you've reached the end of your pathway area, turn around and walk back, again sprinkling the powder with the same hand as you go. This will mark the other side of the path. Now test out your pathway by walking back and forth on your marked out area. Is it wide enough for you to walk comfortably? Do you feel crowded or impeded anywhere? What needs changing? You will probably want to move the lines a bit— widen a corner, move the path over some inches on one side or another, or make other minor changes. Just scuff away the powdery marks that you don't like, and re-mark those spots again. Keep going back and forth, modifying the lines until you are totally pleased with the walking-

flow of the pathway in both directions AND like the way it looks. I often sprinkle the marking powder half-a-dozen times, going back and forth, to make sure I have it right.

After you are happy with the results, you need to mark the area with something more permanent than a powder. It doesn't take much to lose the white lines if people or animals walk over the area, plus rain or sprinklers will wash them away. Also, in time, the lines simply vanish into the earth.

You can temporarily use spray-paint made for marking the ground, which will stay put for a while, but a semi-permanent marking system is crucial. I have developed a system that has always worked well for me:

On hard or firm ground, I use the wide green-colored plastic garden tape (that is available in garden centers everywhere), along with 3-inch nails to hold down the tape, and a hammer. There are two techniques that work well. The first outlines the entire path, and the second

marks it in "dots," that you can connect when you are ready to actually construct the path.

This first technique allows me to see the path completely outlined with the green tape. I can then shovel the area to raise, lower, or level out the soil, if necessary, for a real feel of the finished path.

Simply roll out the plastic tape over your powdery lines, and nail it down with your 3-inch nails into the ground, using your hammer. Pound the nails all the way into the ground, for safety. That's it! Your path is marked.

The second method is good if you don't want to see lines of green tape strung along the ground; have animals, people, or equipment in the area that might trip over the strands of tape or rip them out of the ground; or you don't plan to construct the path for a while and prefer to have the markings more inconspicuous.

Use pieces of plastic tape cut about 2-inches long. Tack the tape pieces into the ground at regular intervals along the length of your outline, using a nail in the center of each piece. Hammer the nails all the way into the ground. Place the tape pieces close enough together that you will be able to redraw your lines in the future, using the green dots as guides. You will need to place them close together around curves, but can have them spread many feet apart on straightaways. You will then connect these dots with a fresh powdery or painted line when you are ready to construct the walkway.

Note:

With either of these methods, PLEASE let any equipment operator know you have nails in the ground, as nails *can* puncture tractor tires. If you think a flat tire on a car is a hassle, just imagine changing and repairing a tractor tire ten times that size! Also, if anyone will be crossing over your marked-out area, and your ground is soft or sandy, you may want to make a wide space free of nails to allow people, and a wheelbarrow or garden cart, a safe zone for passage.

Step Design

When building steps I use a simple formula that I learned from an article about the world-famous architect Alan Blanc, who had a lifelong obsession with steps and stairways. The stairways designed by Alan and Sylvia Blanc, both architects, are thrilling works of art and precision.

As George Washington Carver did with pathways, Alan Blanc learned by watching people —only he watched them walk up and down stairs. He noticed that in some locations many people would trip on the steps—with everybody tripping at the same spot. Other stairways, people would pass up and down without mishap.

Why is this? Steps have an ideal ratio between the rise and distance between each step. If the ratio is off between the two, then you have steps that people are likely to trip on. Steps need to accommodate the natural walking pattern of our bodies. The article gave a simple formula for building steps that people can climb and descend with ease.

The magic number for his formula is 26. This number, 26, relates to the height of the rise (how many inches tall each step is), and depth of the tread (the flat area where you step). To figure out the ratio using this number: First, double the number that is the height of the rise (a 5 1/2-inch rise will give you 11 inches when doubled). Then, subtract that number (11 inches, in this example) from

the number 26, and you get 15—which is how deep the tread should be for the step. This means:

—A 3-inch rise should have a 20-inch tread
—A 3 1/2-inch rise should have a 19-inch tread
—A 4-inch rise should have an 18-inch tread
—A 4 1/2-inch rise should have a 17-inch tread
—A 5-inch rise should have a 16-inch tread
—A 5 1/2-inch rise should have a 15-inch tread.
—A 6-inch rise should have a 14-inch tread.
—A 6 1/2-inch rise should have a 13-inch tread

*Standard rises inside a house usually range from 6 1/2 to 8 inches. Don't use a rise higher than 8 inches, because it puts too much strain on your knees, hips, and ankles.

Doing the actual layout of a stairway is more complex, allowing for landings, distances involved, width of steps, and so on. But the basic rise and tread will give you a terrific head start. One additional pointer is, if your stairway is curved, make your measurements for the treads near the middle of each step, or where people will be walking.

Steps in the garden should reflect the feeling of a relaxed, leisurely stroll, making a short rise to a step especially nice. A 5 1/2-inch rise gives a pleasant, easy feeling (and works well with lumber sizing), but anything up to a 6 1/2-inch rise is delightful.

For a woodland or informal stairway, you may like using flat rocks set into the slope for your steps, rather than a more structured stairway. Just use the stair formula with the rocks, and space them measuring from the front edge of each one.

Now, I must warn you that EVERY builder I've worked with has argued with me when I ask them to use this formula of Alan Blanc's. Sometimes the argument includes, "But it's only for steps in a garden!" as though steps outdoors don't matter. It seems that most builders haven't heard of this formula before, nor do they understand its importance. The builders' usual argument is they think the tread should not be *deeper* with a short rise—figuring that with a 4 1/2-inch rise you want a short tread, also (which is the opposite of Blanc's formula). But I always remain adamant that the stairs be modeled after Alan Blanc's system. The resulting steps and stairways turn out to have a natural flow that makes them a joy to use. Alan Blanc was a genius with stairways, and his wisdom is worth following—even in the garden.

Zones: And Other Facts You'll Need to Know

As wonderful as it might be to buy any tree, flower, or shrub that local nurseries offer, that is not always feasible. Learn what zone you live in (someone in your local garden nursery should be able to tell you), the elevation of your garden, and any particulars about your site.

You need to know the mini-climate of your landscape, so you can design your garden to provide all your plants with the best possible growing conditions. In a hilly or mountainous region, it makes a difference if you are on the edge of a snow-zone, or if fog settles around your property more than it does in other areas. Summertime heat is more intense with full southern exposures, whereas on a north slope, cold can be a problem. Learn from which direction the prevailing winds and storms in winter will blow, and the direction of summer breezes. Conditions such as a windy landscape will limit your selection of plantings, for strong winds will shred delicate leaves.

Find someone in your local nursery who is knowledgeable, and has worked with plants, locally, for years. It's nice to have someone who can answer your questions and offer good suggestions about buying and caring for plants. It takes years to acquire knowledge about plants, where they grow well, where they have problems, plant diseases, and what tends to happen in your region.

A few pointers:

—If you live in a snow zone, do not plant trees or shrubs under the eaves of your house, where melting snow sliding off the roof can break branches and crush plants that lie below.

—If your site is windy, read about which shrubs, trees, and flowers can handle the beating winds. Also work with ways to protect areas with fences, walls, or screens, or by using plants as a hedge or screen to shield areas of your garden. Even wind caused by steady traffic along a main road is enough to destroy some flowers. Learn what you can before you plant! Winds also sap the moisture from plants (just as winds dry out our skin), so plants that like a moist environment will not do as well.

—Heat or Drought. If lack of water is a problem in your area, learn about which plants need a lot of water, and which ones do fine with less. Plants native to your region are good choices.

—Plant names: Latin is the universal language for plants. The nice part is that in any country

the same name is used. The difficult part is for the homeowner or novice gardener who is suddenly hearing Latin. *The Sunset Garden Guide* is a fabulous reference source. You can look up the common name for a plant and are then referred to the Latin name. Listed under each (Latin) plant name are the varieties available, the zones where they are likely to grow well, and general soil or growing conditions that may be required.

Nancy Mair is a professional landscape designer and part of a team of artisans specializing in custom home renovation throughout Northern California. Nancy is also an accomplished chef and the best-selling author of books on cooking and conscious living. She is the recipient of the Outstanding Achievement Award in landscape design by the California Landscape Contractors Association.

Few people have the diverse background that Nancy Mair has: she has been a professional skier, hot air balloon pilot and flight instructor, construction foreman, advanced first aid trainer, and volunteer firefighter. Nancy lives and works with her husband, Kerry, near Nevada City, California.

Nancy Mair offers consulting services to individuals, contractors, and corporations for both landscape and home design. If you are interested in finding out more about either Nancy or her professional services, please visit her website at:

www.nancymair.com or contact her at nancy@nancymair.com

Also by Nancy Mair:

The Spirit of Cooking (Fall 2005)
*Simply Vegetarian! Easy-to-prepare recipes
    for the vegetarian gourmet*
*Grace—freeing the swan within for a
    beautiful life*
*Intimate Vegetarian—Delicious Practical
    Recipes for Singles and Couples*

Other books from Crystal Clarity:

By J. Donald Walters:

Secrets for Women
Secrets of Love
Secrets of Inner Peace
Secrets of Comfort & Joy
Intuition for Starters
Affirmations for Self-Healing

By Jyotish Novak:

30-Day Essentials for Marriage
30-Day Essentials for Career
30-Day Essentials for Wellness

For more information, to request a catalog, or place an order for a book from Crystal Clarity, please contact us at:

Crystal Clarity Publishers
14618 Tyler Foote Road
Nevada City, Ca 95959

Toll Free: 800.424.1055 or, 530.478.7600
Fax: 530.478.7610
clarity@crystalclarity.com

For our online catalog and secure ordering, please visit us on the web at:
www.crystalclarity.com